Ruby Bridges

History Maker Bios

Madeline Donaldson

LERNER PUBLICATIONS COMPANY • MINNEAPOLIS

To Joseph, Madeline, and Clare,
who make me proud to be their aunt

Lerner Publications Company
A division of Lerner Publishing Group, Inc.
241 First Avenue North
Minneapolis, MN 55401 U.S.A.

Website address: www.lernerbooks.com

Library of Congress Cataloging-in-Publication Data

Donaldson, Madeline.
    Ruby Bridges / by Madeline Donaldson.
        p. cm. — (History maker biographies)
    Includes bibliographical references and index.
    ISBN 978–0–7613–4220–5 (lib. bdg. : alk. paper)
    1. Bridges, Ruby—Juvenile literature. 2. African Americans—Louisiana—New
Orleans—Biography—Juvenile literature. 3. School integration—Louisiana—
New Orleans—Juvenile literature. 4. New Orleans (La.)—Race relations—
Juvenile literature. I. Title.
F379.N553B753 2009
379.2'63092—dc22 [B]   2008046526

Manufactured in the United States of America
3 – VI – 11/1/10

TABLE OF CONTENTS

INTRODUCTION

First-grader Ruby Bridges kept her eyes looking forward. She was walking into William Frantz Public School in New Orleans, Louisiana, on November 14, 1960. It was her first day of school.

She was dressed in crisp, white clothes. Her mother walked with her. Mrs. Bridges looked straight ahead. Police officers called U.S. marshals surrounded them.

Ruby and her mom weren't in trouble. The marshals were protecting them. Ruby was doing something brave. She was going to be the first African American to go to William Frantz. Some white people didn't want her to go to the school. They shouted hateful words. They wanted to scare Ruby away. But she kept looking ahead. She was determined to finish first grade.

This is her story.

1 THE WAY THINGS WERE

R uby Nell Bridges was born in Mississippi on September 8, 1954. Her grandparents were farmers called sharecroppers. This meant they didn't own their land. They gave the landowner a share of their crops as rent. Ruby's parents, Abon and Lucille Bridges, worked on his parents' farm. The work was hard.

Sharecroppers work
farmland in the
South in the 1940s.

After Ruby was born,
Lucille and Abon wanted to
find a better way to make a living. In 1958,
they decided to move to New Orleans,
Louisiana. Both Mississippi and Louisiana
are part of the southern United States.

Times were hard for black people in the South. They didn't enjoy full civil rights. What are these rights? Imagine you wanted to take a drink from a water fountain. But the one nearest you had a sign that said you couldn't drink from it. Why? Only white people were allowed to use this fountain.

Black people and white people had to use separate drinking fountains.

In New Orleans, black students had to go to separate schools in the 1950s.

What about eating in a restaurant? If you were African American, you couldn't go into some diners. A sign said you wouldn't be served. What if you couldn't go to a public school in your neighborhood because of your race? People should have the right to do these things, no matter what their religion or gender or race is. All these rights are civil rights.

Civil rights activists speak out against separate, unequal schools.

When Ruby was born, people called activists had already been working hard to bring civil rights to all Americans. One way to get civil rights is through legal action. By going to court, civil rights activists help make it against the law to take away civil rights.

In 1954, the U.S. Supreme Court—the country's highest court—said it wasn't lawful to keep African Americans from going to whites-only schools. The Court said these schools must integrate. This means that black children and white children—in fact, all children—could enroll in the same schools. But integration was slow to happen in the South.

BROWN V. BOARD OF EDUCATION

Local laws and customs blocked efforts to integrate schools. Several civil rights groups took this problem to court. Eventually, the U.S. Supreme Court heard a case called *Brown v. Board of Education*. It said that black children weren't getting an equal education. Because they couldn't go to good schools—the ones only white children could attend—they were getting a poorer education. The Court ruled that separate schools for blacks and whites were unlawful. The ruling stated that schools must integrate.

2 SMALL GIRL, BIG JOB

Ruby's family settled in the Ninth Ward, a poor section of New Orleans. The family had grown. Ruby was the oldest. She had two brothers and a sister. Her father worked in a gas station. Her mother got different jobs to make money. Ruby went to church and to an all-black kindergarten. She played with other African American children on her block. She helped her mom care for the little ones.

By early 1960, a new U.S. law said New Orleans had been too slow to integrate its schools. J. Skelly Wright, a U.S. court judge, said schools had to integrate by September. By chance, that's when Ruby would start first grade.

This school in Baltimore, Maryland, integrated right after the court ruling. Schools in Louisiana did not.

A civil rights group called the National Association for the Advancement of Colored People (NAACP) was working to integrate New Orleans's schools. One plan was to start by integrating first grade with just a few black children in a couple of schools. But which African American children should be the first to go to these schools? The school board chose to test dozens of black kindergartners, including Ruby. The test was hard to pass.

The NAACP fights for civil rights across the country. This office is in Detroit, Michigan.

Before Ruby, only white students went to William Frantz Public School.

Folks from the NAACP visited the Bridges family. They told Ruby's parents that she had done well on the test. She had been chosen to go to William Frantz Public School. It was a whites-only school near their house in the Ninth Ward.

Abon Bridges was worried that white protesters (ABOVE) would hurt his daughter. Lucille Bridges believed Ruby would be safe and the cause was worth it.

Lucille Bridges had strong views about education. She wanted her daughter to have a chance to get good schooling. Lucille felt a better education gave a person better choices for jobs later on. Abon Bridges wanted his daughter to be safe and happy. He didn't want her to go to a school where she might be in danger. But Lucille convinced Abon to let Ruby start first grade at William Frantz.

Most white people in New Orleans were against integration. They kept making new laws to stop it from happening. That worked for a while. Then Judge Wright set a final date for integration—November 14, 1960. On that day, four black girls would integrate two schools. Three first graders would go to McDonogh elementary school. Ruby would integrate William Frantz alone.

U.S. marshals walk with two of the girls at McDonogh elementary school in November 1960.

INTEGRATING ELSEWHERE

African American students in other parts of the South had been integrating schools too. In 1957, nine black teenagers had braved crowds in Little Rock, Arkansas, to go to an all-white high school. White parents and others who were against integration shouted at them. But the teenagers had protectors. U.S. Army soldiers surrounded them as they entered the school. Bravely, the students kept showing up, and they finished the school year.

Elizabeth Eckford (in sunglasses) was one of the teenagers who integrated an all-white high school in Little Rock, Arkansas, in 1957.

$$2 + 2 = 4$$
$$3 + 3 = 6$$
$$4 + 4 = 8$$

3 FIRST GRADE

Judge Wright wanted to make sure
Ruby and the other girls would not be
harmed. He asked U.S. marshals to take
them to and from school each day. Lucille
got Ruby ready for her first day at the new
school. "I want you to behave yourself
today and do what the marshals say,"
she said. "There might be a lot of people
outside this new school. But you don't need
to be afraid. I'll be with you."

The marshals drove them to William Frantz. White people crowded outside. They shouted mean words at Lucille and Ruby. That first day, mother and daughter stayed in the principal's office. White parents arrived to take their children out of the school. By the end of the day, only a few white children were left.

U.S. marshals went to school and home from school with Ruby for much of first grade.

The next day, Lucille and Ruby returned to William Frantz. This time, a young white teacher named Barbara Henry met them. She was from Massachusetts. Mrs. Henry led them to her classroom. Lucille stayed in the back. Ruby sat at a desk in the front. No other children were in the classroom. And that's how it stayed for most of the year.

MRS. HENRY

Barbara Henry came to New Orleans when her husband got a job there. She had taught at schools in other parts of the world. She hoped to teach in New Orleans. When the first grade at William Frantz was ordered to be integrated, the first-grade teacher there quit her job rather than teach a black child. The head of the city's schools called Mrs. Henry to offer her the job. The other teachers avoided her. Sometimes she felt just as alone as Ruby did.

Barbara Henry (shown in 2007) sits at a copy of the desk in her classroom at William Frantz.

After those first days, Ruby went off to school alone, with the marshals. She was very brave. She walked through the angry crowd, which still shouted at her. Mrs. Henry often gave Ruby a hug when she arrived. They worked on lessons together.

Ruby was smart, and she got all Mrs. Henry's attention. She did very well in school. She also grew to love Mrs. Henry, who loved her in return. Mrs. Henry later said, "She was an extraordinary little girl. . . . She was strong enough to counter all the obstacles that were put in her way." Charles Burks, one of the marshals, later said, "She never cried. . . . She just marched along like a little soldier."

This photograph shows Ruby around the time she started at William Frantz.

Another person helped Ruby through first grade. He was Dr. Robert Coles, a child psychiatrist. Dr. Coles gave Ruby a chance to talk about what was going on. He asked her to draw pictures to show how she felt. The extra attention made Ruby feel special. Dr. Coles later said, "Ruby had a will. . . . She possessed honor, courage."

Ruby drew this picture of herself in school for Dr. Coles.

Ruby and her family lived in the Ninth Ward. The families in the Ninth Ward helped them.

Ruby's school year was hard for the Bridges family. Her father lost his job. Her grandparents were told to move off the land they had farmed. But people in the Ninth Ward supported the Bridges family. A man who owned a house painting company gave Abon a new job.

Many white people protested outside the school. Ruby's mother told her to pray for them.

When Lucille had to go to work, other women helped Ruby get ready for school. Neighbors walked along as the marshals drove her to school. And the Bridges family also felt the strength they got from their faith. Lucille encouraged Ruby to pray. She told her especially to pray for the white people who shouted at her. Ruby did this every day.

By the end of the school year, a few white children had returned to William Frantz. Some of them were first graders. They had a different teacher than Ruby had. But sometimes, they came to Mrs. Henry's class for lessons. Sometimes, Ruby played with them at recess.

A few white children continued to attend William Frantz in the fall, but most didn't return until the spring.

The angry crowd was gone. The marshals no longer took Ruby to school. Her first year at William Frantz ended quietly. When asked later how she'd done it, Ruby said that "getting through first grade was partly just a matter of obeying my parents."

4 GROWING UP

Ruby found second grade very different from first. Lots of kids—black and white—went to William Frantz. She had a different teacher. Mrs. Henry was going to have her first child. So she had moved back to Massachusetts.

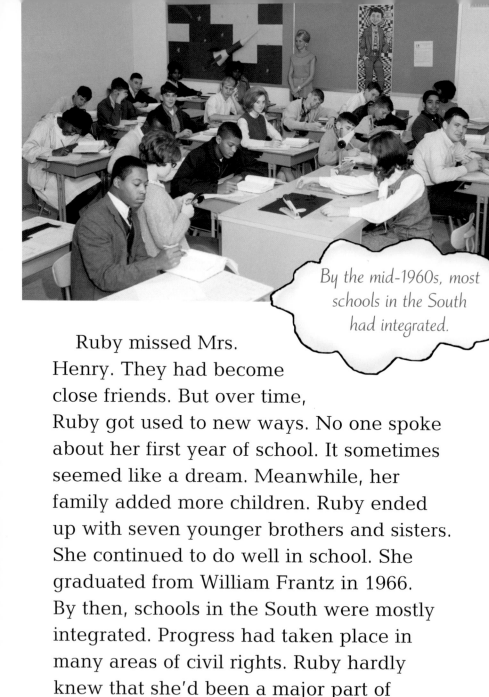

By the mid-1960s, most schools in the South had integrated.

Ruby missed Mrs. Henry. They had become close friends. But over time, Ruby got used to new ways. No one spoke about her first year of school. It sometimes seemed like a dream. Meanwhile, her family added more children. Ruby ended up with seven younger brothers and sisters. She continued to do well in school. She graduated from William Frantz in 1966. By then, schools in the South were mostly integrated. Progress had taken place in many areas of civil rights. Ruby hardly knew that she'd been a major part of that progress.

About this time, her parents divorced. They had never really agreed on giving Ruby such a heavy load at such a young age. Lucille moved the family to a different house. Ruby's father stayed in their old house in the Ninth Ward. Ruby missed her father. She was used to seeing him every day.

THE NINTH WARD

The Ninth Ward is a section of eastern New Orleans. It lies between Lake Pontchartrain and the Mississippi River. Raised barriers called levees are designed to protect the Ninth Ward from flooding when the river overflows or when storms hit the city. The people of the Ninth Ward are mostly African American. Most own their own homes. The community includes many historic homes and churches, as well as some of the best musicians in the United States.

Ruby went to an integrated high school in New Orleans. She graduated in 1972. Her dream was to go to college. But the family couldn't afford to send her. Instead, Ruby studied travel and tourism. She got a job as a travel agent. Eventually, she worked for American Express, a company that deals in international travel. She became one of its first African American travel agents in New Orleans. Through her job, Ruby was also able to see the world beyond New Orleans.

Ruby worked for American Express. The company helps people travel all over the world.

This portrait shows Ruby in the early 1980s.

While going after her career, Ruby also began a serious relationship with Malcolm Hall. They dated for several years and married in 1975. By the 1990s, they were raising four sons. The family didn't have much money. Ruby's sons went to integrated schools in New Orleans. She focused on raising them. Not many people knew that Ruby Hall was Ruby Bridges. And Ruby herself seemed to separate the two parts of her life.

Then, a tragic event made her remember her past. In 1993, her youngest brother, Milton, was killed in a drug-related murder. For a time, his four daughters lived with Ruby and Malcolm. The girls were students at William Frantz.

After many years, Ruby returned to the school she had integrated in first grade.

Ruby went back to the school she had helped integrate. What she found surprised her. Instead of a racially mixed group of students, all the students were black. The school was falling apart. It lacked after-school activities, such as dancing and music classes. Its school library was in bad shape. Didn't parents and neighbors care about the school?

Ruby realized that she had kept her focus too close to home. She volunteered at William Frantz. She talked to parents. She worked with the local community. Together, they arranged after-school activities at William Frantz. Through this work, Ruby found a second chance to make a difference.

5 FACING FORWARD

Ruby knew she wanted to focus on education, children, and family. She wanted to get parents involved again. And she wanted to end racism. But she wasn't sure how to begin. Then, in 1995, her old friend, Dr. Coles, published *The Story of Ruby Bridges*. This picture book showed the world what Ruby had gone through as a first grader. He used the money he earned from telling Ruby's story to help Ruby set up a new organization.

With this money, Ruby was able to set up the Ruby Bridges Foundation in 1999. Its vision is to end racism in all its forms. One of the foundation's first programs was called Ruby's Bridges. Its mission is to bring together children of different backgrounds.

Ruby reads THE STORY OF RUBY BRIDGES to a first-grade class in New York.

Schools from different parts of the same city are paired. The students become pen pals. They go on field trips together. Sometimes, they work together in their communities. Ruby feels strongly that children can teach fairness and kindness to one another and to adults.

REINTRODUCING RUBY

Many years had passed since Ruby had seen Mrs. Henry. In 1996, TV host Oprah Winfrey brought them together. They talked about their experience on *Oprah*. In 1998, Disney aired a TV movie about Ruby's first year at William Frantz. *Ruby Bridges* gave kids and grown-ups a way to understand Ruby's courage. In 1999, Ruby wrote her own book about her experience called *Through My Eyes*. These events introduced Ruby again to children and adults across the United States.

Ruby speaks at charity events and meetings across the country. Sometimes she talks about her book, THROUGH MY EYES (LEFT).

To help send that message far and wide, Ruby travels around the country. She speaks at schools, churches, lunch meetings, and conventions. She talks about her experience and what it taught her. She reminds people that no one can judge another person simply by how they look.

But Ruby still had more work to do. In August 2005, Hurricane Katrina struck New Orleans. The levees broke. Water flooded the Lower Ninth Ward. The water crashed through, rising more than twenty feet high. The flooding flattened the ward. People lost their homes. Schools, including William Frantz, closed. The offices of the foundation closed too.

Hurricane Katrina destroyed much of the Lower Ninth Ward.

All the schools in the Lower Ninth Ward were damaged by the floodwaters.

Through her foundation, Ruby had become known outside New Orleans. She used her fame to tell people what was going on in the Ninth Ward after Katrina. She joined with other nonprofit groups to make people aware of the need to rebuild.

Some people focused on housing. But Ruby focused her energies on rebuilding schools. Progress has been slow. As of mid-2008, only a few schools in the Lower Ninth have reopened. Many kids in the area, if they go to school at all, have to travel across town. But Ruby isn't giving up. She believes education and helping families are the keys to bringing back the Ninth Ward.

The Samuel J. Green Charter School was one of the first schools in New Orleans to reopen after Hurricane Katrina.

Ruby Bridges went through something extraordinary. But she isn't just a symbol. She's a real person who still believes in education and community. She is still committed to making racism a thing of the past. As Ruby says, "Racism is a grown-up disease. Let's stop using kids to spread it."

TIMELINE

RUBY NELL BRIDGES WAS BORN ON SEPTEMBER 8, 1954, IN TYLERTOWN, MISSISSIPPI.

In the year . . .

1954 The U.S. Supreme Court rules on *Brown v. Board of Education.* The court says black and white children have the right to go to the same schools.

1960 Ruby starts first grade at William Frantz Public School. Age 6

1964 Norman Rockwell depicts Ruby in his painting *The Problem We All Live With.*

1966 Ruby graduates from William Frantz. Age 11

1972 Ruby graduates from high school. Ruby enters business school to learn the travel and tourism industry.

1973 Ruby starts working as a travel agent.

1975 Ruby marries Malcolm Hall. Age 21

1993 Ruby's youngest brother, Milton, is killed.

1995 Dr. Robert Coles publishes *The Story of Ruby Bridges.* Ruby receives an honorary college degree from Connecticut College.

1996 Ruby is reunited with Mrs. Henry on *Oprah.* Age 42

1998 Disney shows *Ruby Bridges* on TV.

1999 Ruby writes *Through My Eyes.* Ruby sets up the Ruby Bridges Foundation. Age 45

2001 Ruby receives the Presidential Citizens Medal.

2005 Hurricane Katrina destroys parts of New Orleans, including the Ninth Ward, where Ruby grew up.

2009 *Ruby! The Story of Ruby Bridges* is presented by the SteppingStone Theatre in Saint Paul, Minnesota. Age 55

THE PROBLEM WE ALL LIVE WITH

Beginning in the early 1900s, U.S. painter Norman Rockwell created American scenes. His paintings were often printed on the cover of the *Saturday Evening Post*, a weekly magazine. Most of the time, the scenes were upbeat. They showed an ideal, mostly white, mostly small-town America. And that's what the *Post* wanted. It pressured Rockwell only to show African Americans and other minorities working for white people.

In 1963, after more than forty years of making cover art for the *Post*, Rockwell stopped. He started working for *Look* magazine. His very first cover made people think. He created *The Problem We All Live With*. It showed a little African American girl surrounded by grown-up men. She was passing a wall that held a hateful word that people called African Americans.

The girl in the artwork was Ruby. She didn't know until she was grown that Rockwell had painted it. Ruby's mother, Lucille Bridges, saw the real painting for the first time in 2006 *(right)*. After Katrina, she'd been evacuated from New Orleans to Houston, where the painting was on loan.

FURTHER READING

Bridges, Ruby. *Through My Eyes.* **New York: Scholastic, 1999.** Ruby gives her own account of her experience in this special book.

Coles, Robert. *The Story of Ruby Bridges.* **New York: Scholastic, 1995.** This picture book introduced Ruby to a whole new group of kids and parents.

Lucas, Eileen. *Cracking the Wall: The Struggles of the Little Rock Nine.* **Minneapolis: Millbrook Press, 1997.** This illustrated book tells the story of the nine teenagers who helped integrate a high school in Arkansas in 1957.

Weidt, Maryann N. *Rosa Parks.* **Minneapolis: Lerner Publications Company, 2003.** This biography covers the life of Rosa Parks—another African American woman who took a bold step in the fight for civil rights.

WEBSITES AND DVD

African American World for Kids
http://www.pbskids.org/aaworld/
At this site, kids can play games and learn more about important African Americans.

The Ruby Bridges Foundation
http://www.rubybridgesfoundation.org
Through pictures and articles, Ruby reminds people of her story.

Ruby Bridges: A Real American Hero. DVD. Hollywood, CA: Walt Disney Home Entertainment, 2004. The DVD of the TV movie brings Ruby's brave actions to life.

SELECT BIBLIOGRAPHY

No adult biographies have been published about Ruby Bridges.

Coles, Robert. *Children of Crisis: A Study of Courage and Fear.* Boston: Little, Brown and Co., 1967.

Coles, Robert. *The Moral Life of Children.* New York: Atlantic Monthly Press, 2000.

Hall, Ruby Bridges. "The Education of Ruby Nell," *Guideposts,* March 2000.

Online NewsHour. "A Class of One: A Conversation with Ruby Bridges Hall." *PBS.org.* February 18, 1997. http://www.pbs.org/newshour/bb/race_relations/jan-june97/bridges_2-18.html (February 17, 2009).

Patterson, James T. *Brown v. Board of Education: A Civil Rights Milestone and Its Troubled Legacy.* New York: Oxford University Press, 2002.

Reckdahl, Katy. "Ruby Bridges and Ruby Hall," *Gambit Weekly* (New Orleans), June 8, 2004.

Renwick, Lucille. "The Courage to Learn," *Instructor,* August 1, 2001.

Steinbeck, John. *Travels with Charley and Later Novels 1947–1962.* New York: Library of America, 2007.

INDEX

Acknowledgments

The images in this book are used with the permission of: © Bettmann/CORBIS, pp. 4, 8, 13, 15, 16, 23, 26, 27, 33; Library of Congress, pp. 7 (LC-DIG-fsac-1a33894), 14 (LC-USZ62-33783); © Robert W. Kelley/Time & Life Pictures/Getty Images, p. 9; © National Archive/Newsmakers/Getty Images, p. 10; © Donald Uhrbrock/Time & Life Pictures/Getty Images, p. 17; © Francis Miller/Time & Life Pictures/Getty Images, p. 18; AP Photo, pp. 20, 32; AP Photo/Kokomo Tribune, Tim Bath, p. 22; Drawing by Ruby Bridges from CHILDREN OF CRISIS—VOLUME I by ROBERT COLES. Copyright © 1964, 1965, 1966, 1967 by Robert Coles. By permission of LITTLE, BROWN & COMPANY, p. 24; Louisiana Division/City Archives, New Orleans Public Library, p. 25; © Jack Moebes/CORBIS, p. 30; Photo by Kathy Anderson © 2009 The Times-Picayune Publishing Co., all rights reserved. Used with permission of The Times-Picayune, p. 34; AP Photo/Tina Fineberg, p. 37; © Rick Mackler/Globe Photos, Inc., p. 39; AP Photo/Kevork Djansezian, p. 40; © Chris Graythen/Getty Images, p. 41; REUTERS/Lee Celano, p. 42; AP Photo/Houston Chronicle, Steve Ueckert, p. 45. Front Cover: © Bettmann/CORBIS. Back Cover: © photos_alyson/Taxi/Getty Images.

For quoted material: pp. 19, 24, 28, Ruby Bridges. *Through My Eyes* (New York: Scholastic, 1999); p. 23, Lucille Renwick. "The Courage to Learn." *Instructor*, August 1, 2001; p. 23, Online Newshour. "A Class of One: A Conversation with Ruby Bridges Hall." *PBS.org*. February 18, 1997; p. 43, Ruby Bridges. "Official Webite." *Ruby Bridges*, 2004, http://www.rubybridges.com/book.php (February 10, 2009).